Shells on the Sand Shells in the Sea

A Young Person's First Guide to North Atlantic Seashells

Frances B. Haviland

To my family,
the wonder of shells,
and the magic of childhood.

Many thanks to the following young shell collectors of Nantucket Island, Massachusetts; Vermont; New Hampshire; New York; New Jersey; Maryland; and Connecticut:

Mike, Matthew, Aileen, Kelsey, Colin, Wyatt, Lily, Eric, Jonathan, Preston, Ashley, Emma, Rachel, Maria, Vicki, Ben, and David

Special thanks to:

Eric A. Lazo-Wasem
Division of Invertebrate Zoology
Senior Collections Manager
Peabody Museum of Natural History
Yale University
New Haven, Connecticut

James C. Widman Jr.
Research Fishery Biologist, NOAA
National Marine Fisheries Service
Milford, Connecticut

Acknowledgments:

Special thanks to Sam Haviland for expert assistance with image inventory,
to Barbara Beekley Meyers for educational advice,
and to Lee Rand Burne for editorial assistance.

Library of Congress Control Number: 2005903738
ISBN 10: Softcover 1-4134-9066-2
Hardcover 1-4134-9067-0

ISBN 13: Softcover 978-1-4134-9066-4
Hardcover 978-1-4134-9067-1

This book was printed in the United States of America.

To order additional copies of this book, contact:
Xlibris Corporation
1-888-795-4274
www.Xlibris.com
Orders@Xlibris.com

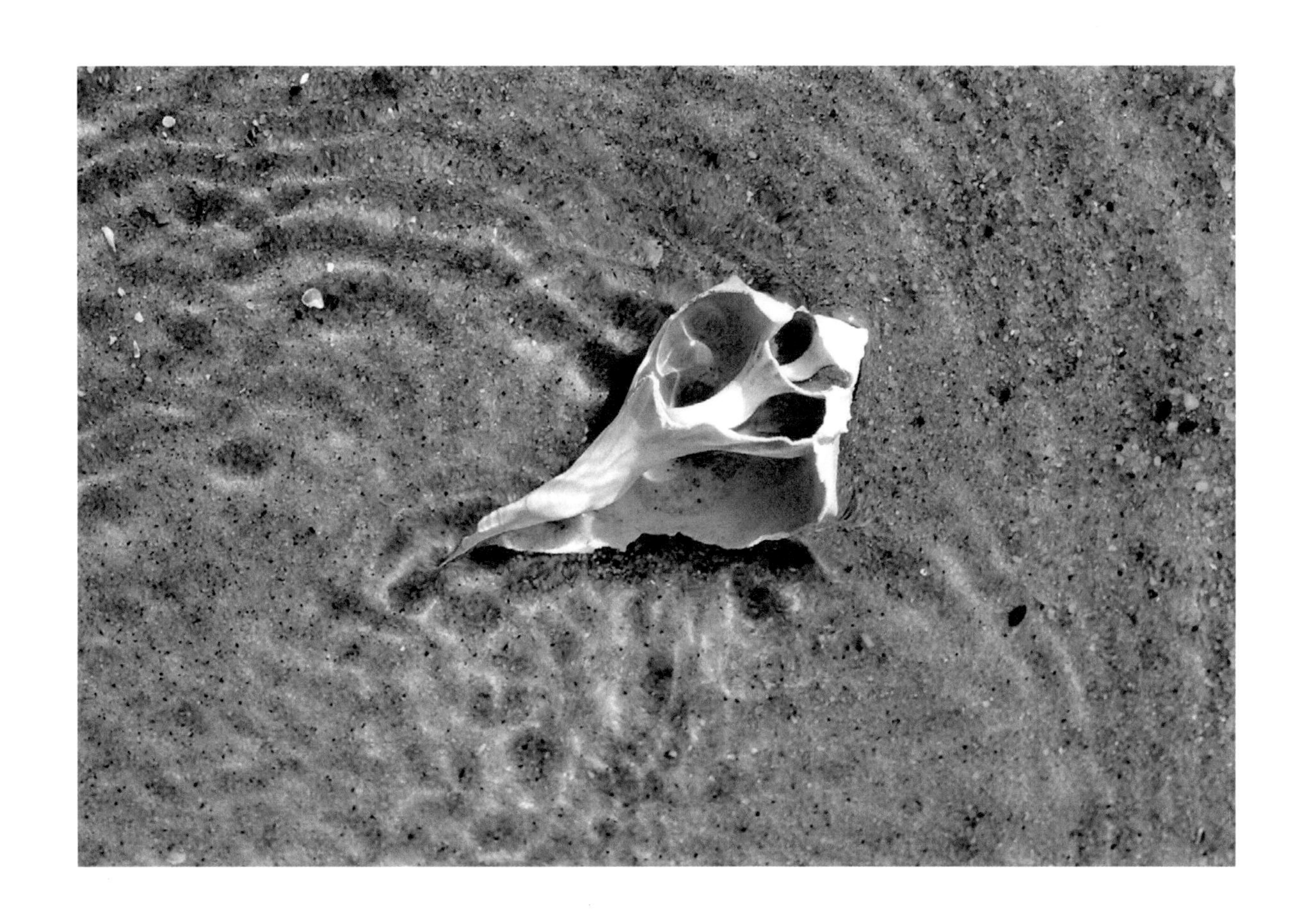

Shells on the sand

were once shells in the sea.

Soft animals called mollusks
were once living in those shells in the sea.

Mollusks have no backbone.
They are called invertebrates.

Mollusks are the second largest group of animals (insects are the largest group).

Mollusks have been used for food since ancient times. Their shells have been used for religious symbols, jewelry, tools, and musical instruments in many cultures around the world. And they still are today.

"Sailor's Valentine"
created by David Rhyne,
Sarasota, Florida

Shell Art provided by The Conch House
Stonington, Connecticut

A live whelk, at low tide, pushes sand ahead of itself like a bulldozer, searching for food.

Scientists divide mollusks into five groups. We will look at the two most common groups: gastropods (one shell) and bivalves (two hinged shells or valves).

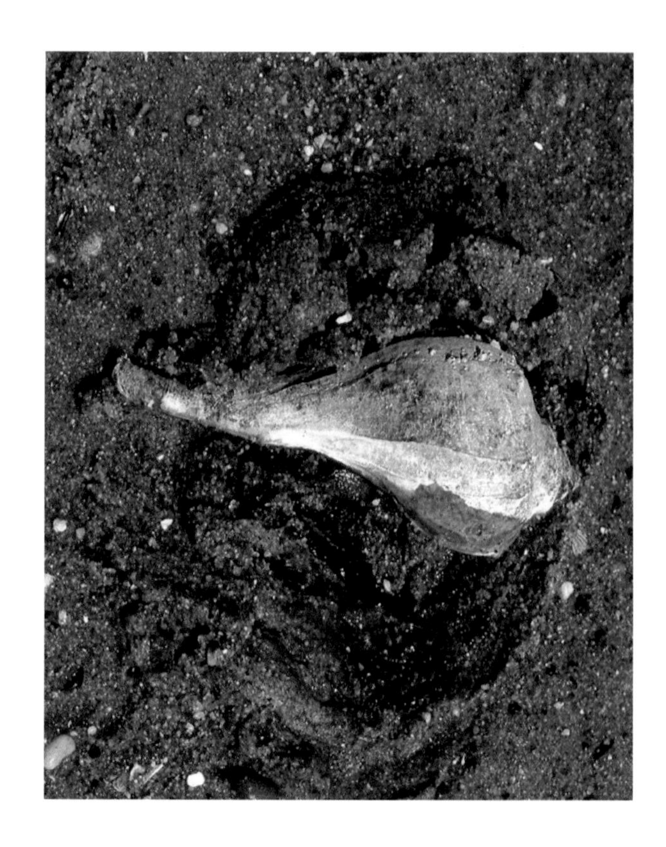

A person who collects and studies shells is called a conchologist. To be one you will need a curious mind – and a pail for the beach. You will need a shell guide and a notebook for record keeping, and you should learn the best times and places to find shells.

First, you should learn about tides. The pull of gravity, between the moon and the earth, causes ocean changes up to four times each day. The water comes in twice and goes out twice each day. The water level recedes for six hours, exposing the beach, until it's finally low tide.

Then the water level rises again for six hours, gradually covering the beach, until it's finally high tide. Then it happens all over again! Because the orbit of the moon changes, the times of the tides will be a few minutes different each day.

Low tide is the best
time to find shells left
by the sea on the sand.

Can you imagine why a low tide after a storm might be even better?

Second, you should know about beaches. The part of the beach between the tides is called the littoral zone, or the intertidal zone.

Sometimes it is covered with water and sometimes it is dry. Usually there are more different kinds of plants and animals there than in many other parts of the ocean. Why do you think it would be hard for plants and animals to stay alive there?

Some baby mollusks begin life without their shells, as tiny larvae. They swim defenseless with their millions of brothers and sisters in the sea. Searching for safe, hard places to land, most of them are eaten by other sea animals. The ones that survive soon begin to make protective shells.

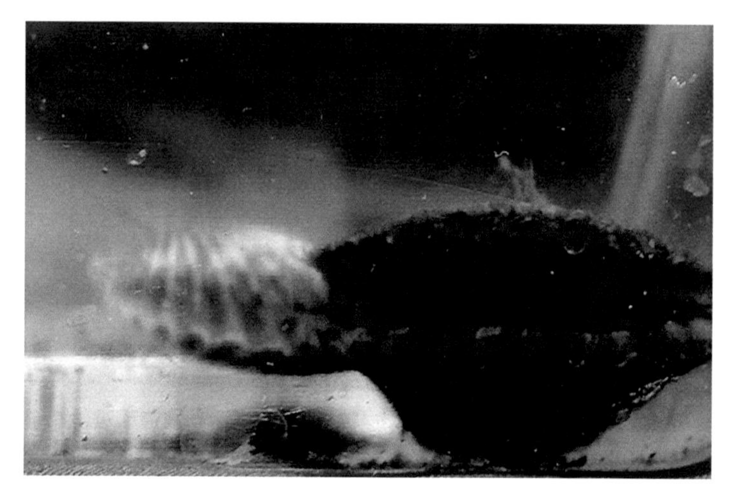

This is done with a special shell-building layer of tissue called the mantle. It covers almost the whole soft animal. The mantle secretes calcium carbonate that hardens to make the shell. Each variety of mollusk has its own unique design. Sometimes, if you are lucky, you can see the mantle at the outer edge of the shell.

The mantle also secretes material to make bright colors and patterns. This means that many shells are smooth and colorful on the inside.

But most shells have different kinds of rough outsides. The tropical cowrie is different. Its mantle extends to the outside, where constant secretion keeps it smooth and glossy. Do you see the shiny cowrie and the rough whelk?

The largest class of mollusks is the class Gastropoda (Greek meaning "stomach foot"). Four common North Atlantic mollusks belonging to this class are whelks; moon snails; slipper, or boat, shells; and periwinkles. They have one spiral-shaped shell, which usually spirals to the right around a center axis. They are univalves. They have a head; eyes; tentacles, or feelers; and a relatively large muscular "foot."

A live moon snail

A left-spiral shell is a real treasure. (But, then, some species of tropical gastropods always spiral left!)

Some gastropods are enemies of bivalves. They move freely about the ocean floor. They extend their large stomach foot ahead of them, searching for plants or animals to eat.

Some gastropods can scrape off algae with a saw-like tongue (radula), drill shells, then suck or tear out the meat!

If you find a shell with a hole in it, you'll know perhaps some gastropod had a feast!

On a string or bright ribbon, these particular shells become a nice bracelet, necklace, windchime, or holiday ornament.

A living whelk is the largest and hardest gastropod to find on the beach.

Hungry gulls usually get it first!
An early morning low tide is the best time to find one.

Many gastropods have hard plates that exactly fit the opening in their shells. It is called an operculum. The mollusk can close it like a trapdoor, to protect itself. These flat, brown, oval-shaped objects are sometimes found separately on the sand.

The knobbed whelk (see the knobs on its shell?) makes an interesting egg case for its babies. If you find a dried “rope” of them on the sand, break open one segment and see many perfectly formed tiny whelks.

If the egg case had stayed in the sea, the babies would have eaten their way out! See the little holes?

The channeled whelk (see the channel, or groove, in its shell?) makes the same sort of egg case, but each segment has only one seam instead of two at the edge. Can you see the difference?

The deep-water waved whelk makes a round egg case about the size of an orange.

In the days of the whaling ships, these were called “seawash balls,” as they are as rough as sandpaper when dry. Whalemen used them to wipe greasy whale fat (called “blubber”) off their hands!

Northern moon snails are voracious enemies of bivalves, drilling shells and tearing away meat. They encase their eggs in sticky mucus, which binds sand grains into a perfect, delicate "collar." If you ever find one in shallow water, leave it where you find it, as you must never take a living specimen. If it's dried on the sand, handle it extremely gently. It's a fragile treasure!

Marine snails called periwinkles are among the smallest gastropods found in North Atlantic waters. They live on rocks among tidal pools.

The easiest gastropods to find are slipper shells, also called boat shells. They attach to each other and to rocks or other shells. They take on the curve of that object. So sometimes they are fairly flat and sometimes really curved.

The flat ones make the best boats. Try to float some in a small tidal pool or dish of water. What do you think will happen?

The second largest class of mollusks is the class Bivalvia.

Clams, mussels, oysters, scallops, and jingle shells are in this class. They are bivalves. Most hinged shells can close completely, using one or two muscles.

Closing the shells protects the soft animal inside from storms and enemies.

Mussels attach themselves to shoreline rocks, jetties, or seaweed.

The thin, strong threads attaching them are called byssus. Byssal threads look like a fuzzy green or black beard. When the tide goes out, bivalves close to keep moisture in. Mussels are easy to gather at low tide. Blue mussels from nonpolluted waters are good to cook and eat. Wear old sneakers on the rocks, and take a grown-up and a pail. Most bivalves live in or on sand or mud, or attached to rocks or seaweed. In contrast to univalves, they usually don't move very far.

Clams take in food and water through one siphon. A second siphon expels waste and water. Clams dig into sand or mud. It's fun to dig soft-shell, or steamer clams.

They burrow fast by means of their long "hatchet foot."

If you step on the sand, they spout water and tell you where they are.

You need to be quick with your hands, a spade, or a clam rake!

Native Americans used mollusks for many things besides food. They cut the slim core of the whelk shell into white wampum (money).

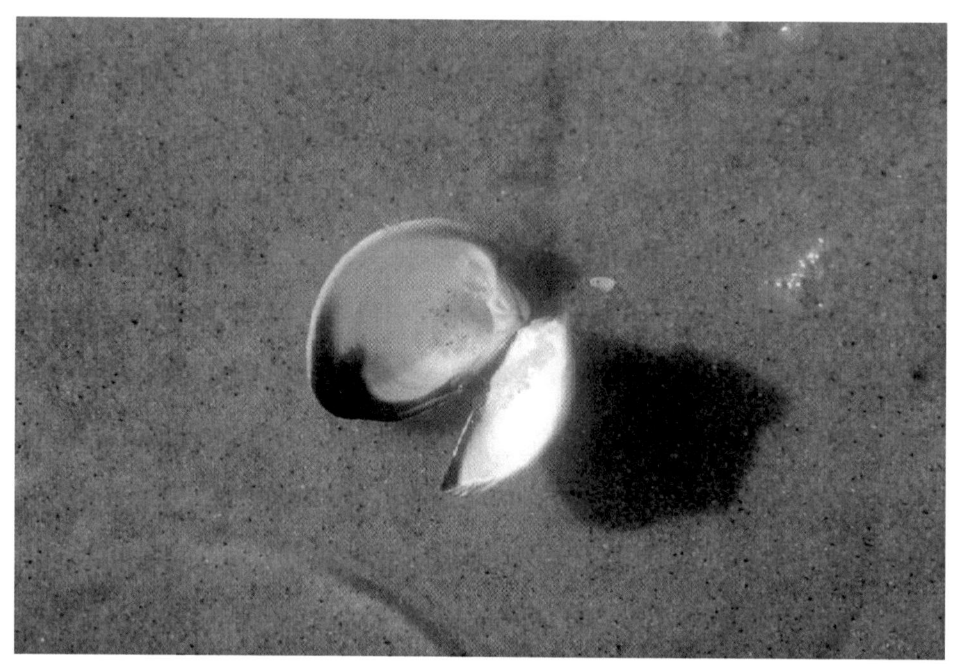

The purple part of the inside edge of the quahog (hard-shell clam) made the most valuable wampum. Native Americans made beaded jewelry and belts with it for trading and also for binding treaties. Jewelry and many other useful decorative things are made from all kinds of shells today.

Jingle shells, or angels' toenails, are thin as leaves, and are found in iridescent colors of gold, pink, silver, and black. They have one rounded shell. The other is flat with a hole at the hinged edge, where its byssus once attached it to rocks or other shells.

Oysters can grow in relatively shallow water, such as Chesapeake Bay and Long Island Sound. Soft baby oysters are called "spat" after they settle.

The babies swim about looking for hard places to lodge. If they land in mud they die, so people who work with oysters spread tons of empty oyster and clam shells on the sea bottom. This is called cultch.

It takes three-to-five years for an oyster to grow big enough (about four inches) to be harvested. Oysters are favorite food all over the world.

Valuable pearls in oysters are found in the coastal waters of Japan, Australia, and the South Seas.

A grain of sand gets between the mantle and the shell and is an irritation. The soft animal covers it with layers of shell material called nacre. Nacre forms around the sand grain until it becomes a pearl! Pearls are rarely found in American oysters and quahogs. Sometimes they are quite pretty and valuable.

Scallops are the only bivalves with eyes (see them along the edge of the live mollusk—lots of beautiful blue ones). Unlike other bivalves, a scallop can move about in an entertaining way. It can swim wherever it wishes! A scallop opens its shell, takes in water, then snaps shut. This jet-propels it in jumps, loops, and swirls!

There are hundreds of different kinds of scallops of many colors and sizes around the world. Consequently, the scallop design appears in many ways in our everyday life.

Now you know some things
about univalves and bivalves,
the two largest classes of mollusks.
Now you know some things
about tides and beaches.
Would you like to be a collector?
You would?
Then get your pail,
take off your shoes,
and let's go to the beach!

INDEX
and
GLOSSARY

INDEX

• Channeled whelk page 19
• Clam page 7, 25, 26
•Jingle shell (or angel's toenail) page 27
• Knobbed whelk page 18

INDEX

• Moon snail page 21
• Periwinkle page 21
• Mussel page 24
• Slipper shell page 22
• Scallop page 30
• Oyster page 28
• Waved whelk page 20

Glossary—Words Shell Collectors Should Know

antennae	Feelers or tentacles in the head of the univalve mollusk.
aperture	Opening in univalve shell.
bivalve	Mollusk with two hinged shells.
Bivalvia	Second largest class of mollusks—two hinged shells.
byssus	Fine, strong, silky threads that anchor mussels, some clams, and possibly other bivalve groups, to rocks or each other.
calcium carbonate	Calcium of lime that mollusk gets from its food and water. Shell-building material.
cephalopod	Mollusk with eight or more arms or tentacles. Most cephalopods have no obvious shell.
conch	Gastropod used for food, tools, jewelry, and musical instruments in many cultures around the world.

conchologist	One who collects and studies shells.
cultch	Empty oyster and clam shells spread by people who work with oysters. The empty shells create the firm base baby oysters need in order to grow.
detritus	Particulate matter that accumulates on the bottom of shallow saltwater marshes and lagoons.
ebb tide	The ocean moving away from the shore, the period between high water and the next low tide.
flood tide	The ocean coming into the shore, the period between low water and the next high tide.
Gastropoda	Largest class of mollusk: one shell- periwinkle, moon snail, conch, and whelk are common ones. One usually coiled shell, eyes, tentacles, radula, “foot,” and mantle.
intertidal	The area of beach between the marks of low and high tides.
littoral	The region of shoreline between high tide and low tide which is sometimes covered with ocean water and sometimes dry.

malacologist	One who collects and studies mollusks and shells.
mantle	Shell-building layer of thin skin that lies between the body and shell and covers most of the soft body of the mollusk. Material from the mantle (mostly carbonate of lime the mollusk gets from its food and water) that hardens to form the shell.
mollusk	A member of the phylum Mollusca.
nacre	Shell-building material (mother-of pearl).
neap tide	When difference between high and low tide is least. Sun and moon form a right angle with the earth. Occurs twice each month.
oceans	Five bodies of water all connected, covering two-thirds of the earth's surface with salt water. Atlantic, Pacific, Indian, Arctic, and Antarctic.

operculum	A tough plate which can be pulled, like a trap door, into the opening (aperture) of a snail's shell, to give it protection.
pelecypod	Name from the Greek meaning "hatchet foot." Bivalve mollusk: clam, oyster, scallop, mussel, jingle("angels' toenails").
phylum	A categorical term below level of kingdom, and above level of class.
phylum Mollusca	Soft-bodied invertebrate (lacking a backbone), typically with a shell for protection and a foot for locomotion. (Mollusca comes from the Greek word *molakus* meaning soft.)
quahog	Large hard-shell clam with purple edge inside shell. Native Americans used them for food, tools, wampum (money), beads to make belts, and jewelry for trading. Still popular today for food and jewelry.
radula	Flexible, file-like tongue of gastropod. Typically used to scrape algae from hard surfaces. Oyster drills, a small subset of radula-possessing gastropods, are expert at drilling into bivalves!

sessile	Referring to an organism that "stays put" at a certain stage of life (in plants, once they have taken root; in animals, typically after the larvae "settle").
spat	Baby oysters after larval stage when they have settled onto a hard place on the bottom of the sea.
spring tide	When difference between low and high tides is greatest. Earth, moon, and sun are in line with each other. Occurs twice each month.
tide	Rise and fall of ocean waters up to four times a day.
univalve	Mollusk with one shell, usually spiral shaped. Some common ones are boat, or slipper, shells; whelks; conchs; moon snails; and periwinkles.

Can you guess what shell this is?
(It's covered with barnacles!)

It's a moon snail shell!

This is a live moon snail.
What kind of a trail do you think it makes in the sand?

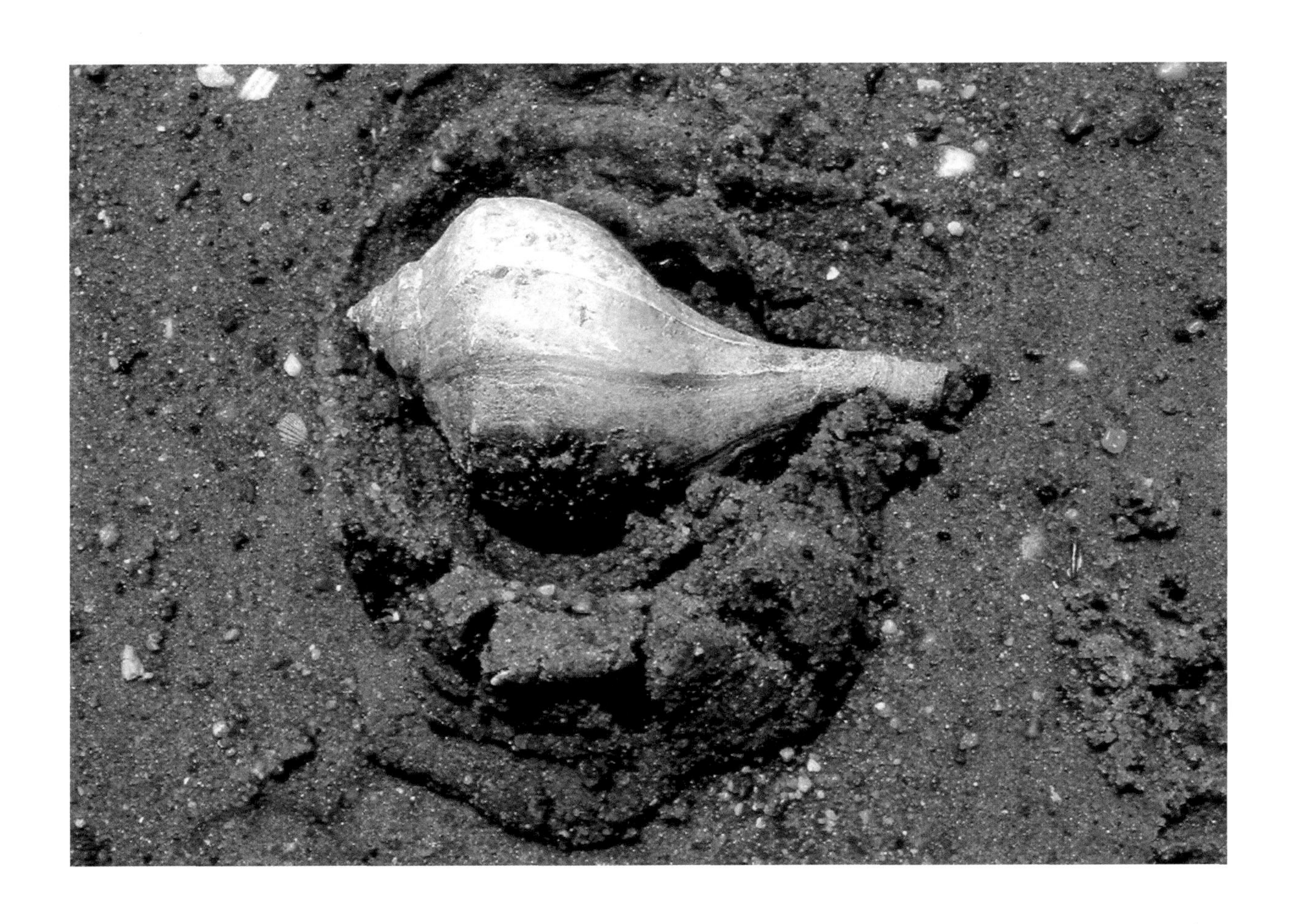

A live knobbed whelk at low tide, rotates in the wet sand, searching for food.